# fast fun & easy®

# FABRIC DYEING

## Create Colorful Fabric for Quilts, Crafts & Wearables

Lynn Koolish

C&T PUBLISHING

Text copyright © 2008 by Lynn Koolish

Artwork copyright © 2008 by C&T Publishing, Inc.

Publisher: Amy Marson

Creative Director: Gailen Runge

Acquisitions Editor: Jan Grigsby

Editors: Karla Menaugh and Kesel Wilson

Technical Editors: Helen Frost and Robyn Gronning

Copyeditor/Proofreader: Wordfirm Inc.

Cover Designer/Book Designer: Kristy K. Zacharias

Production Coordinator: Casey Dukes

Photography by Luke Mulks and Diane Pedersen of C&T Publishing unless otherwise noted

Published by C&T Publishing, Inc., P.O. Box 1456, Lafayette, CA 94549

Library of Congress Cataloging-in-Publication Data

Koolish, Lynn.

 Fast, fun & easy fabric dyeing : create colorful fabric for quilts, crafts & wearables / Lynn Koolish.

  p. cm.

 Summary: "Dye fabric with only a minimal amount of time, effort, and supplies. Fast, uncomplicated dyeing methods without extensive recordkeeping and complicated dye mixing."—Provided by publisher.

 ISBN 978-1-57120-508-7 (paper trade : alk. paper)

 1.  Dyes and dyeing, Domestic. 2.  Dyes and dyeing—Textile fibers.  I. Title.

 TT853.K66 2008
 746.6'041--dc22
                              2008006262

Printed in China

10 9 8 7 6 5 4 3 2

# Dedication

To my husband, Glen—you make it possible for me to keep doing what I love to do.

To my mother, Ruth—you're a great role model for staying healthy, active, and creative.

# Acknowledgments

Almost everyone I know who dyes fabric learned either the basics or more advanced techniques from others. These are the four people from whom I have learned.

I took my first dyeing class from Sonya Lee Barrington. Her class introduced me to the basics and got me started.

Ann Johnston has written and published several books on dyeing that many consider essential, especially when you have a little experience under your belt. Her low-water immersion techniques greatly helped me expand my dyeing horizons.

Jane Dunnewold is known for the concept of complex cloth—layers of color, pattern, and texture that result in fabrics that stand on their own as works of art. Her classes and books are outstanding.

When it comes to more advanced dyeing techniques, Sue Benner is a master. Her Expressive Dye Painting class opened my eyes to a whole new world of dyeing.

I am indebted to all four. They are great teachers and artists who generously share their extensive knowledge and expertise.

Thank you also to the following individuals and companies.

Those who have contributed quilts and other projects:

Helen Frost, Becky Goldsmith, and Laura Wasilowski

Companies that provided materials and information:

Dharma Trading, for dyes, supplies, and cotton fabrics

Duncan Enterprises, for Tulip dyes

Jacquard, for dyes and other supplies

Kaufman Fabrics, for cotton fabrics

Pro Chemical & Dye, for dyes, supplies, and cotton fabrics

RJR Fabrics, for cotton and silk fabrics

Everyone at C&T, for their ongoing support and encouragement.

# Contents

# introduction

This book is designed to help you start dyeing with a minimal investment in terms of time, effort, and supplies. If you already know the basics, you will find some new approaches and techniques.

There are many ways to dye fabric. I've experimented and adapted methods to find the ways of working that fit my needs.

☐ Fast: I generally use methods that don't take a lot of time or effort. I want to dye the fabric and start using it.

☐ Fun: I dye fabric for myself because it's fun, so I don't want to get bogged down by complicated methods, time-consuming techniques, or extensive record keeping.

☐ Easy: I always have dyeing supplies on hand, but because I dye sporadically, I don't want to keep mixed dyes or other solutions around. I mix what I need when I need it. I also use the minimum amount of supplies to get the job done.

In addition to dyeing fabric to make quilts, garments, and other projects, I have learned that it's just as easy to dye clothes, household goods, and other things I already have. In my house, anything that is light colored or stained is a prime candidate for dyeing. I routinely dye clothing, as well as faded bath towels, spotted kitchen towels, stained linen tablecloths and napkins, and more.

So what are you waiting for?

# basic supplies

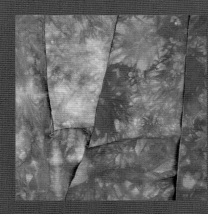

Getting started with fabric dyeing is so easy. All you need are a few supplies, a measuring spoon, a few plastic containers, and some fabric.

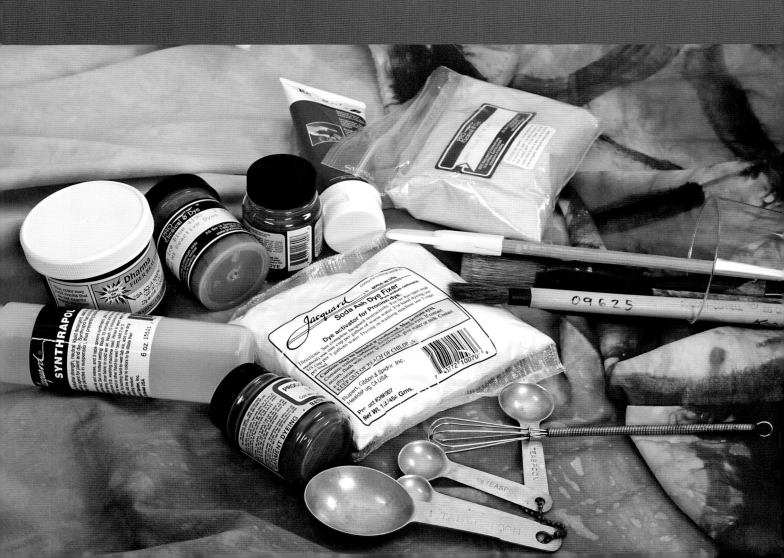

# Supplies

You don't really need very much to get started dyeing. The essentials are dye, fabric, and soda ash. The supplies are easy to find and easy to use.

Basic supplies for dyeing

## dyes

This book is about using Procion MX dyes. They are also called fiber-reactive dyes because the dye forms a permanent bond with the fabric—the color becomes part of the fabric. When properly fixed with soda ash, the dye is colorfast and will not wash out. In fact, your dyed fabric will probably be more colorfast and washfast than most commercial fabric.

Procion dyes can be used on all natural fibers—cotton, rayon, linen, ramie, hemp, silk, and even wool.

The dyes are readily available, are safe to work with, and are used at room temperature with warm water.

## soda ash

Soda ash, also known as sodium carbonate or dye activator, is used to fix the dyes, making the color permanent.

## fabrics

You have many choices when selecting fabric to dye. Dyeing does not change the hand or feel of the fabric, so buy good-quality fabric that you like the feel of. If you are dyeing for the first time, you may think you should use cheap fabrics because you are just experimenting. But cheap fabrics often don't take the dye well, so you are likely to be disappointed. It's better to buy good-quality fabric and experiment by using smaller pieces. Your dyed fabric is only as good as the fabric you start with.

### COTTON

Any 100% cotton fabric can be dyed as long as it is not permanent press or treated with stain-resisting finishes. Buy cottons for dyeing from a quilt or fabric shop or from a source that specializes in fabric that is ready to dye, called PFD—prepared for dyeing (see Resources, page 63).

PFD means that the fabric was not finished with any chemicals or coatings that will inhibit the dyeing process, so the fabrics can be used immediately. If you are not sure whether a fabric is PFD, prewash it (see Prewashing Fabric, page 7).

Another term you will come across is "mercerized." Mercerization is a treatment in the manufacturing process that adds luster to the fabric, making it stronger and more receptive to dyes. Mercerized cotton will give you slightly brighter colors and more distinct textures and patterns. Whether you choose mercerized or nonmercerized fabric will depend on what's available and what you want your dyed fabric to look like. If you are specifically aiming for sharp, crisp textures, mercerized cotton will be your best bet, but any good-quality cotton fabric will yield good results. Different cotton fabrics will take dyes differently, so buy a small quantity of several different types of fabric and try them out.

Different cottons take dye differently. From left to right: unbleached muslin, bleached muslin, broadcloth, pima

# fun!

Commercially printed cotton fabrics can also be dyed (see Mixing Dye Colors, page 18). The results are variable and can be very interesting. If you have fabric you don't like anymore or if you can't find a fabric to fit a specific need, try dyeing over fabric you already have.

## RAYON, LINEN, RAMIE, AND HEMP

Cotton is a plant fiber, and so are rayon, linen, ramie, and hemp. All plant fibers can be dyed in the same way. Colors will be different on each different fiber.

## SILK

Silk is a protein fiber and can be dyed just like cotton, or it can be dyed with vinegar and steamed in the microwave (see Dyeing Silk and Wool, page 53).

## WOOL

Like silk, wool can be dyed with vinegar and steamed in the microwave (see Dyeing Silk and Wool, page 53).

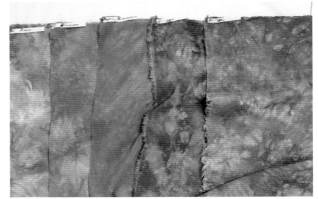

One dye, different fabrics. From left to right: raw silk, silk habotai, cotton-silk voile, rayon, linen

# prewashing fabric

If you are not sure whether your fabric is PFD, wash it with hot water and detergent or Synthrapol (see Synthrapol, page 8) before dyeing. Do not use fabric softener. If you want to start dyeing with dry fabric, either hang the washed fabric to dry or put it in the dryer. Do not use dryer sheets.

# easy!

Keep track of how different fabrics dye by dyeing them in the same dye bath. Be sure to mark them with pins and beads so you know which fabric is which (see page 13). After rinsing and drying, pin on a label identifying the type of fabric, and keep them on hand for future reference.

# other helpful supplies

Other supplies

## SYNTHRAPOL

Synthrapol is used as both a prewash to remove substances that can interfere with dyeing and as an afterwash to help keep the loose dye in suspension so it can be washed away without staining other areas of the fabric.

## SALT

Salt is used to achieve an even color when dyeing solid colors (see Mostly Solid Dyeing, page 21). Salt helps push the dye into the fiber.

## SODIUM ALGINATE

Sodium alginate is used to thicken dyes for direct applications such as painting (see Applying Dye Directly, page 42).

## WATER SOFTENER

If your water is hard, you may want to use a water softener (see Resources, page 62).

## REDURAN

Even when you wear gloves and are very careful, you will get some dye on your skin. If you plan to do much dyeing, getting a tube of ReDuRan, a dye and stain hand cleaner, is a good idea. It's best to use it immediately after you come in contact with the dye, rather than waiting.

# Tools

Tools for dyeing

You need only a few basic tools. Just remember that once you've used them for dyeing, you should never use them for anything else.

## measuring and mixing tools

Here's what you need in the way of tools:

- ☐ Set of measuring spoons for measuring dye powder and soda ash
- ☐ Wire whisk for mixing
- ☐ Plastic spoons for mixing
- ☐ Small rubber spatula for getting thickened dye out of containers
- ☐ Dust masks
- ☐ Rubber gloves

## containers

Household buckets, recycled plastic containers, and zip-top plastic bags are perfect for dyeing. Depending on the type of dyeing you want to do and the amount of fabric you want to dye, you might want to use 5-gallon buckets, 1-gallon buckets or plastic bottles with the tops cut off, quart-sized yogurt containers, or 6- to 8-ounce yogurt or cottage cheese containers.

# Where to Buy Dyeing Supplies

Procion MX dyes and the other needed supplies are readily available from a number of sources.

Many art supply stores sell dyes made by Jacquard in a ⅔-ounce size for $3 to $5, depending on the color. If you've never dyed before, this can be an easy way to try it. If a store carries the dyes, it should also carry the soda ash that you need to fix the dyes. Jacquard has a website with information and ideas (see Resources, page 62).

The two other primary sources for Procion MX dyes and everything else you could possibly need to dye fabrics are Dharma Trading in California and Pro Chemical & Dye (known as ProChem) in Massachusetts. Both have extensive and informative websites and catalogs (see Resources, page 62). Dharma and ProChem sell the Procion MX dyes starting in 2-ounce containers and sell larger quantities as well. Their 2-ounce containers range in price from about $4 to $7, depending on the color.

Each company has its own color names and numbering system, so Golden Yellow from one company isn't the same as Golden Yellow from another company. Refer to each company's color charts to select colors.

There is another set of dyes, called Procion H, which works differently. When you buy dyes, be sure to get the MX dyes.

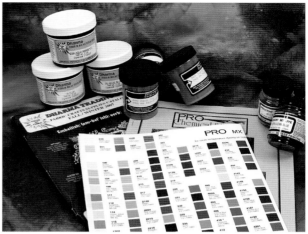
Dyes are easy to find.

# What Colors Should You Buy to Get Started?

Procion MX dyes come in a wide range of colors. Some dyers suggest buying just a few colors and then mixing everything else. My suggestion is to start with colors you like. If there is a premixed color you want to use, it's easier to buy it rather than mixing it up each time (see Color, page 15).

# basic
# techniques

There's really no wrong way to dye fabric. Have fun trying new colors and techniques to create your own unique fabric.

# Mixing Dye Solutions

Dyes are sold as a powder that you mix with water to create the dye solution. Each dyeing method in this book includes recommended amounts of dye powder, soda ash, and water. Use the recommended amounts as a starting point, and refer to this chapter for the mixing techniques. As you gain experience, you'll be able to judge the amount of dye powder you need for the effect you are trying to achieve and the fabric you are using. For extremely dark colors, you'll need to increase the recommended amount of dye powder.

## easy!

If a piece of fabric doesn't come out as dark as you would like, just dye it again with the same color.

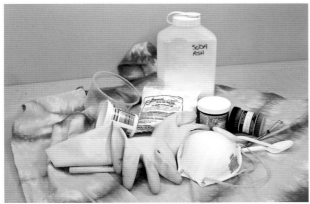

Tools for mixing dyes

## Safety First

Always wear gloves when working with dyes—even when rinsing fabric.

Always wear a dust mask when working with dye powders.

## dye powder

To create the dye solutions, mix the recommended amount of dye with warm water. Use just enough water at first to dissolve the dye powder. It's important to make sure the dye powder is *completely* dissolved; otherwise you will get spots of concentrated color on your fabric. To mix dyes, use a spoon, a small wire whisk, or a plastic container with a lid that you can shake. Then add the remaining amount of water as directed for each dyeing method.

## fast!

Plastic condiment squeeze bottles are great for mixing and applying dyes. Ones with wider openings make it fast and easy to add the dye powder and soda ash. Screw the lid on tight, and shake to dissolve the dye.

## soda ash

Soda ash (or dye activator) is essential for fixing the dyes. There are three methods for getting the soda ash into the process. Refer to each dyeing process for the amount of soda ash to use.

### □ MIX THE SODA ASH INTO THE DYE SOLUTION.

This works for all types of dyeing. The soda ash starts to react with the dye as soon as it is mixed in, so you should use the dye solutions within about 30 minutes. For amounts, refer to the charts accompanying the instructions for each dyeing process.

### □ PRETREAT FABRIC IN A SODA-ASH SOAK.

Use this method with any type of dyeing. It is especially appropriate when you don't want to have to worry about using the mixed dyes right away or when you are working with a group (see fun!, page 20). When you use soda-soaked fabric, you don't need to mix soda ash into the dye solutions. The soda-soak solution is reusable and will keep indefinitely, so you can keep it on hand.

### Soda-Soak Recipe

1. Mix 9 tablespoons of soda ash into 1 gallon of warm or hot water. Mix well to make sure all the soda ash is dissolved.

2. Soak your fabric for about 20 minutes in the soda-soak solution.

3. Wring out the fabric and hang it to dry. Do not put the fabric in the dryer. Or, if you are going to use the fabric wet, you don't need to let it dry.

## easy!

When you're finished soaking fabric, pour the excess soda-ash soak back into a storage container, such as a 1-gallon plastic bottle.

### □ ADD SODA ASH AFTER THE DYE HAS BEEN APPLIED.

Some dyers use this as their preferred method. You can use this method if you realize that you've forgotten to add the soda ash earlier.

1. Dissolve the soda ash in warm or hot water. Let the solution cool to room temperature. Use the same amount of soda ash as you would have if you had added it to the dye when starting (for amounts, refer to the charts accompanying the instructions for each dyeing process).

2. Pour the soda-ash solution into the container with the dyed fabric, and let it sit for the recommended amount of time.

## Thickening Dyes

For some techniques, such as direct application (see Applying Dye Directly, page 42) and creating patterns (see Dyeing Patterns, page 47), it helps to thicken the dye before you use it.

1. Mix 1 tablespoon of sodium alginate with 1 cup of hot water.

2. Mix well, making sure all the sodium alginate granules are dissolved. The mixture will be very thick and lumpy, but it will smooth out over time. You want the mixture to be very thick because it will thin out as you mix it with the dye.

It's best to mix the sodium-alginate thickener and let it sit overnight. At a minimum, let it sit for a few hours. Dyers who use a lot of thickened dye often have a blender just for this task. For occasional use, a wire kitchen whisk will do the job.

# Timing

Fiber-reactive dyes need time to react with the fiber and the soda ash. The amount of time depends on the technique you are using. Fabric that is soaking in dye needs a minimum of 2 hours, but you can leave it longer, even as long as overnight. Fabric that has dye applied directly to it needs to sit, or batch, for 12 to 24 hours, but it can sit longer if you can't wash it out within that time frame.

## easy!

If you are dyeing a lot of fabric and need to keep track of colors and timing, write the color and start time on a piece of masking or painter's tape, and tape it to the side of each container you are using.

# Record Keeping

Some dyers keep very detailed recipes and notes. Others do not. If you keep notes, it will be easier to reproduce your results. If you don't keep notes, you may feel freer to experiment and be spontaneous. Do what works for you.

As you are learning, I recommend that you keep samples of dyed fabric and some basic information. After you've been dyeing for a while, you may not want to bother to keep records. Basic information to record includes the following:

☐ The type of fabric

☐ The color(s) of dye used

☐ The amount of fabric, water, dye, soda ash, and salt (if used)

☐ The type of manipulation

☐ The length of time the fabric was in the dye

Keep records as needed.

## fast!

A quick way to keep track of fabric when experimenting is to use colored beads on safety pins to identify different samples. For example, if you are trying three different shades of red, use a different color of bead for each color of dye to track your results. Writing on fabric, even in permanent ink, can get lost in the dyeing process.

# Rinsing and Washing Dyed Fabric

After the dyeing is complete, rinse the fabric in *cold* water first to stop the dyeing process. If you start the rinsing process in hot water, migrating dye may stain other areas of your fabric. Leave the fabric soaking in cold water for 20 to 30 minutes. After the cold-water rinse, wash the fabric in *hot* water and Synthrapol (see Synthrapol, page 8).

You will need to run the fabric through several hot wash cycles to get all the excess dye out of the fabric. Or if you are washing the fabric by hand, a good approach is to leave the fabric soaking for 15 minutes, then rinse. Repeat this process until the water runs clear and you don't see any more color coming out of the fabric.

# easy!

> If you're new to dyeing and don't have Synthrapol, use a liquid detergent such as Dawn dishwashing detergent—just make sure the product you are using doesn't have bleach in it. Use about a teaspoon of either detergent or Dawn for a full washer load or an appropriate portion for smaller loads. If you'll be doing much dyeing, it's worth getting the Synthrapol.

## making sure all excess dye has been washed away

A good way to check whether all the excess dye has been washed away is to iron the wet fabric between two pieces of white fabric. If you see any traces of color, you need to wash the fabric again.

Check to be sure all excess dye is washed away.

# Finishing Up

Wait until your fabric has been completely washed, dried, *and* ironed to decide whether you like it. Until that final step of ironing, you won't know exactly what the fabric looks like. Wet fabric always looks darker than dry fabric, and many subtleties aren't apparent until the fabric is completely dry and ironed.

# fun!

> Some of my favorite dye pieces started as cleanup cloths that I used to wipe up spills, excess dyes, and so on. Always keep a cleanup cloth handy. Start with a white piece of cloth, or use a dyed piece you don't like.

# color

Dyeing is all about color: light, dark, bright, subdued. When you dye your own fabric, you can create any colors you choose.

Once you start dyeing, you'll want to start mixing some of your own colors, combining multiple colors in one piece of fabric, and dyeing over colored fabric. There are books and courses on color theory, but the following will get you started. If color theory is new to you, you'll want to have the 3-in-1 Color Tool (see Resources, page 62) or a color wheel on hand. My advice is to have fun playing with color and try new and unusual combinations that are uniquely yours.

3-in-1 Color Tool and color wheel

# Primary Colors

The primary colors are the basic colors from which all other colors are created: red, blue, and yellow.

# Secondary Colors

The secondary colors are created by mixing two primary colors: violet, green, and orange.

# fun!

Try mixing your own secondary colors from the primary colors: yellow and just a touch of blue will make green, yellow and a touch of red will make orange, and red and a bit of blue will make violet.

# Tertiary Colors

Tertiary colors are created by mixing a primary color and one of the secondary colors next to it on the color wheel: yellow-orange, red-orange, red-violet, and so on.

Color wheel

# Color Schemes

There are many different types of color schemes, but understanding a few basic ones goes a long way. These color schemes help you understand what happens when you mix and blend colors and will give you ideas of colors to use together, either in a single piece of fabric or in multiple pieces of fabric.

### analogous color scheme

Colors that are next to each other on the color wheel are analogous. Analogous colors always go together and blend well, whether you are combining them in one piece of fabric or doing a two-color gradation (see page 38).

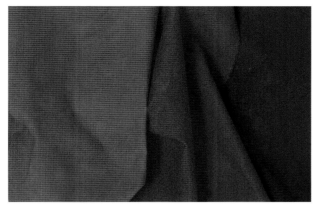
Analogous colors always blend.

## complementary color scheme

Complementary colors are across from each other on the color wheel: red and green, blue and orange, yellow and violet, blue-violet and yellow-orange, and so on. Complementary colors always provide high contrast when placed next to each other. Mixing complementary colors together results in a neutral color, such as brown, gray, or something in between. Sometimes these mixed colors are wonderful; sometimes they are muddy. Combining complementary colors in one piece of fabric can result in a wonderfully dramatic piece, or, if they blend too much, the result can be dull and muddy. When they are used in a two-color gradation (see page 38), you can get a great range of colors. The only way to know for sure is to try them out.

Complementary colors provide strong contrast.

(see page 38)

# easy!

A little bit of a color's complement can be used to tone down the color.

Blue added to orange tones down the color.

## split-complementary color scheme

A split-complementary color scheme uses one color plus the colors that are next to that color's complement. This scheme provides much of the contrast of the complementary colors but is toned down a bit.

Split-complementary colors provide toned-down contrast.

## triadic color scheme

A triadic color scheme uses three colors that are equally spaced around the color wheel. This scheme increases the range of colors used and provides contrast while maintaining balance and harmony.

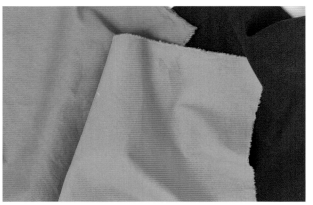

Triadic color scheme provides contrast and harmony.

# Tints, Tones, and Shades

When painting, you can create a tint by adding white to a color. There is no white dye, so you must create tints by using less dye powder or more water to create a lighter color. Adding gray dye to a color creates a tone, and adding black creates a shade.

Tints, tones, and shades of blue-green

Using tints, tones, and shades in dyeing greatly increases the range of options you'll have to use in your quilts and other fabric projects.

## easy!

Using tints, tones, and shades of one color is an easy way to create fabrics for a one-color, or monochromatic, color scheme.

## easy!

Adding a touch of brown to a color is an easy way to soften it while still maintaining the color.

Brown added to red-violet softens the color.

# Mixing Dye Colors

Any of the Procion MX dyes can be mixed together, so even with a limited number of colors, you can mix just about anything you like.

Always start with the paler or weaker color and gradually add the darker or stronger color. For example, yellow is quickly overwhelmed by any other color. If you want to mix a yellow-green, start with the yellow, and add small amounts of green until you get the color you want. If you are adding black to create a shade, add tiny amounts of black very gradually.

There are three ways to mix colors:

- ☐ Mix the colors in the dye solution before you apply the dye. The color will be uniform.

- ☐ Blend wet dyes on the fabric. The color will be mottled, depending on how much you play with the fabric after you apply the dye. This is a great way to produce fabric with interesting mixes and blends of color.

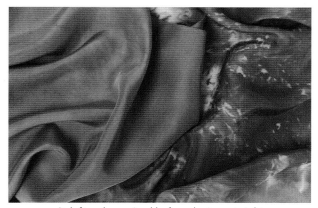

At left, colors mixed before dyeing; at right, colors mixed during dyeing

- ☐ Dye one color over another (overdyeing). The evenness of the color will depend on the original color(s) and how evenly you apply the additional color(s). You can overdye commercially printed fabric or hand-dyed fabric. Dyes are transparent, so the base color of the fabric will affect the final color of your fabric. For example, if you start with fabric that is yellow and overdye it with a light blue, you will get green. When you are overdyeing a single color, it is easy to predict what the new color will be based on basic color-mixing theory (e.g. dyeing a red fabric with blue dye will yield purple).

When overdyeing a print, be sure to look at all the colors in the print, and think about how the new color will affect each one. Overdyeing is a great way to change the color of fabric that you don't like or that doesn't meet your needs.

Original fabrics

Fabrics overdyed with light blue

Fabrics overdyed with peach-orange

You can overdye prints to change overall color.

# easy!

A good way to try out colors is to mix a little dye powder with water and use a paintbrush to paint it on fabric or paper. It won't be an exact match, but it will give you an idea of what the color will look like. This is a good way to mix colors to see what you will get.

Try out colors on paper.

# fun!

In some fabrics, such as white-on-white designs, metallic prints, or black-and-white prints, parts of the design actually resist the dye and produce striking results.

Some printed designs resist dye.

You can overdye solids to add texture.

# fun!

Fabric dyeing is a great activity for groups of all ages. Kids as young as eight can dye fabric under adult supervision, as long as the adult mixes the chemicals for them and the children understand that they must wear masks and rubber or latex gloves and be careful with the dyes. One of the easiest ways to work with groups is to premix the dyes in squeeze bottles and work with soda-soaked fabric or T-shirts (see Soda Ash, page 6) so there are no time constraints on using up the mixed dye.

Tulip dyes work well for group projects because they are premixed. You just add water.

# mostly
# solid dyeing

Hand-dyed fabrics have a luminous glow no matter what colors you use, so even solid colors have a unique look when you dye them yourself.

# What You'll Need

☐  PFD or prewashed fabric (see Cotton, page 6)

## DYEING TIME

☐  2 hours or longer

| MOSTLY SOLID DYEING *AMOUNTS PER 1 YARD OF FABRIC* | | | | |
|---|---|---|---|---|
| | **DYE POWDER** | **SODA ASH\*** | **SALT** | **CONTAINER** |
| Light color | ½–1 teaspoon | 1 tablespoon | ⅓ cup | 5+ gallons |
| Medium color | 1–2 teaspoons | 1 tablespoon | ⅓ cup | 5+ gallons |
| Dark color | 3–4 teaspoons | 1 tablespoon | ⅓ cup | 5+ gallons |

| MOSTLY SOLID DYEING *AMOUNTS PER ¼ YARD OF FABRIC* | | | | |
|---|---|---|---|---|
| | **DYE POWDER** | **SODA ASH\*** | **SALT** | **CONTAINER\*\*** |
| Light color | ¼–½ teaspoon | 1 teaspoon | 4 teaspoons | 1–5 gallons |
| Medium color | ½–¾ teaspoon | 1 teaspoon | 4 teaspoons | 1–5 gallons |
| Dark color | 1–1½ teaspoons | 1 teaspoon | 4 teaspoons | 1–5 gallons |

\* *Either plan to add soda ash to your dye mixture, or use soda-soaked fabric (see Soda Ash, page 6).*

\*\* *For completely solid fabrics, use a 5-gallon bucket for ¼ to ½ yard of fabric, and use the washing machine for anything larger (see Dyeing in a Washing Machine, page 23).*

# How-Tos

I call my solids "mostly solid" because I like to have a little bit of variation in them. For truly solid colors, fill a larger container and stir frequently. For the most evenly dyed solid colors, use a washing machine (see Dyeing in a Washing Machine, page 23).

Why dye your own solid colors?

☐  When you dye your own solid (or mostly solid) colors, you can get any color you want.

☐  Fabrics dyed with Procion MX dyes have a luminous quality that commercially available solid fabrics don't have.

☐  Hand-dyed solids have small variations to break up the surface and give it depth.

# preparation

1. Use PFD fabric (see Cotton, page 6) or prewash your fabric to remove any finishing that may inhibit dyeing. Either plan to add soda ash to your dye mixture or use soda-soaked fabric (see Soda Ash, page 6). Start with wet or dry fabric.

2. Select a container based on the amount of fabric you have. For slightly mottled fabric, use a smaller container (see Mostly Solid Dyeing chart, above). To get a completely even color, the fabric needs to move freely in the dye solution and needs to be stirred frequently. Use a container that is at least as large as the large size indicated in the chart; larger is fine. For the most even color, dye in your washing machine (see Dyeing in a Washing Machine, page 23).

3. Prepare the dye (see Mostly Solid Dyeing chart, page 22, and Mixing Dye Solutions, page 11). Be sure all the dye powder, salt, and soda ash are dissolved.

## dyeing in buckets

1. Put the dye solution, salt, and dissolved soda ash/dye activator into the selected container with enough water to completely cover the fabric. If you are using soda-soaked fabric, you don't need to add soda ash or dye activator.

2. Place the fabric in the dye bath. Stir or agitate frequently, especially for the first hour of the dyeing time.

3. Let the fabric sit in the dye for 2 hours or more before washing (see Rinsing and Washing Dyed Fabric, page 13).

Dyeing in bucket

## dyeing in a washing machine

If you are dyeing a yard or more of fabric or are dyeing thick or heavy fabrics, such as terry cloth or sweatshirt knits, and want a very even color, use a washing machine.

1. Use the lowest water setting that will work for the quantity of fabric you are dyeing. Use a warm wash setting and the longest time setting. Fill the washer and stop the cycle when the tub is full.

2. Mix the dye, salt, and soda ash/dye activator as above. Be sure all the dye powder, salt, and soda ash are dissolved, and add to the washer. Let the machine agitate for a few seconds to mix the dye.

3. Add the fabric, and let the machine agitate for a few minutes.

4. Let the fabric sit for a few minutes, and then agitate again for 30 seconds to a minute.

5. Use the entire wash cycle to alternately let the fabric sit and then agitate briefly. Agitate more frequently at the beginning of the dyeing time.

6. The fabric should be in the dye for at least 2 hours before washing (see Rinsing and Washing Dyed Fabric, page 13).

---

Yes, it's OK to use the same washing machine for dyeing or rinsing as you do for your household laundry. I've done it for years without any problems. After you've used the machine for dyeing, wipe the inside with a light-colored towel or rag. If there are any signs of dye on your rag, rinse out the wash tub. When you are ready to use it for your normal laundry, first run a load of dark-colored clothes or things you don't care about, such as rags or throw rugs.

# Variations

**Completely solid colors dyed in large buckets or washing machine**

**Mostly solid colors dyed in containers**

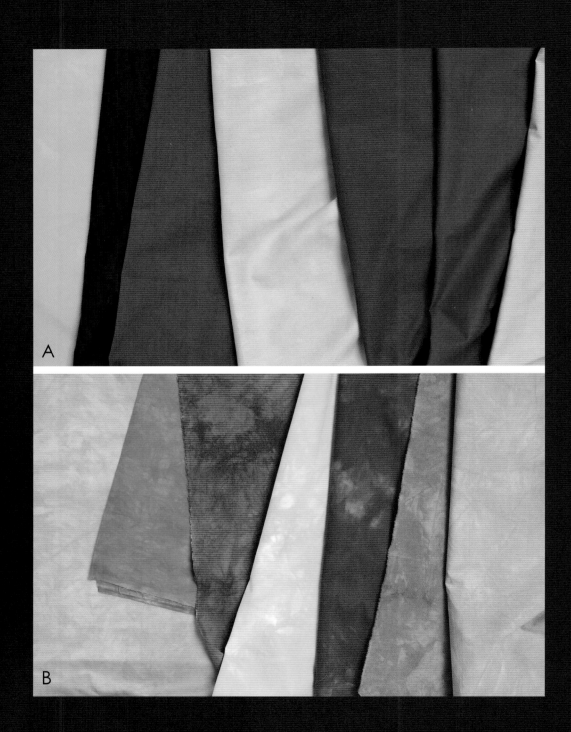

A

B

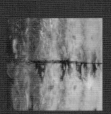

# textured
# dyeing

There's no limit to the types of textures you can create when you dye your own fabrics. Be adventurous and see what you come up with.

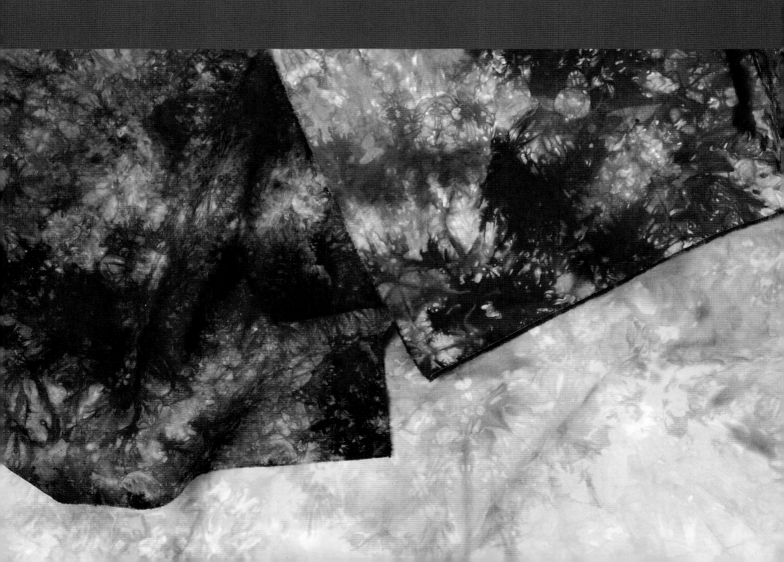

# What You'll Need

☐ PFD or prewashed fabric (see Cotton, page 6)

**DYEING TIME**

☐ 2 hours or longer

| TEXTURED DYEING, LOW-WATER IMMERSION *AMOUNTS PER 1 YARD OF FABRIC* | | | |
|---|---|---|---|
| | **DYE POWDER** | **SODA ASH\*** | **CONTAINER** |
| Light color | 1/2 teaspoon | 1 tablespoon | 1–2 quarts |
| Medium color | 1 teaspoon | 1 tablespoon | 1–2 quarts |
| Dark color | 2 teaspoons | 1 tablespoon | 1–2 quarts |
| TEXTURED DYEING, LOW-WATER IMMERSION *AMOUNTS PER 1/4 YARD OF FABRIC* | | | |
| | **DYE POWDER** | **SODA ASH\*** | **CONTAINER** |
| Light color | 1/8–1/4 teaspoon | 1 teaspoon | 1–2 cups |
| Medium color | 1/4 teaspoon | 1 teaspoon | 1–2 cups |
| Dark color | 1/2 teaspoon | 1 teaspoon | 1–2 cups |
| *\* Either plan to add soda ash to your dye mixture, or use soda-soaked fabric (see Soda Ash, page 6).* | | | |

# How-Tos

These techniques are generally known as low-water immersion dyeing—meaning dyeing fabric with a minimal amount of water. Fabric is generally scrunched into a container, resulting in an amazing array of color effects, textures, and variations. The more tightly the fabric is scrunched, the harder it is for dye to penetrate, giving more visual texture and color variation.

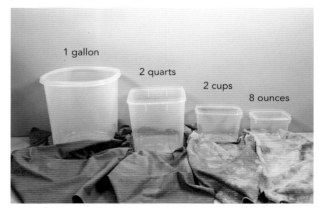

Tighter scrunching = more texture and color variation—
Fabrics were dyed in corresponding containers.

There are so many possibilities with this technique. Scrunching and rolling are just two to get you started. Either method can be applied with one color, two colors, or more than two colors. Two colors or more can be used in one step or in multiple steps. When using two colors or more, be sure to keep in mind how the colors will mix or blend (see Mixing Dye Colors, page 18).

## preparation

1. Use PFD fabric (see Cotton, page 6) or prewash your fabric to remove any finishing that may inhibit dyeing. Either plan to add soda ash to your dye mixture or use soda-soaked fabric (see Soda Ash, page 6). Start with wet or dry fabric.

# fun!

Here's a quick experiment. Prepare two small containers of dye. Scrunch dry fabric into one container and wet fabric into the other container, and see what happens. You'll find the answer later in this chapter (see Wet vs. Dry Fabric, page 31).

2. Select a container based on the amount of fabric you have and the amount of texture you want. The more tightly packed the fabric, the more variation in color and value, so choose your container accordingly. You can use anything from a small yogurt container for a quarter-yard of fabric to a small bucket for several yards of fabric.

# easy!

Zip-top plastic bags work well, but it's a good idea to put them into another container in case they leak.

3. Prepare the dye (see Textured Dyeing, Low-Water Immersion chart, page 26, and Mixing Dye Solutions, page 11).

## scrunching

### SINGLE-COLOR DYEING

1. Simply scrunch fabric into a container, and pour on the dye. For the most distinct patterns and textures, don't touch the fabric. If you want more subtle textures, move the dye around a bit in the container.

2. Let the fabric sit in the dye for 2 hours or more before washing (see Rinsing and Washing Dyed Fabric, page 13).

Scrunch fabric and pour on dye.

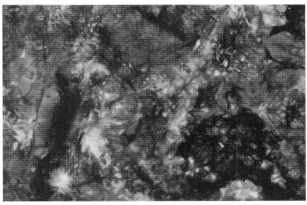

Scrunched fabric dyed with single color

## TWO-COLOR DYEING

When dyeing with two colors, you can choose from several approaches. Use enough dye to saturate the fabric, but not so much so that either color completely covers the fabric.

1A. Pour a little dye into the bottom of the container. Push the fabric into the container. Pour the second color of dye on top of the fabric. At this point you can either leave the fabric alone or move it around a bit to get the colors to mix. With this option, the colors will stay distinct if you don't touch or move the fabric around. The more you move the fabric, the more the colors will blend.

Pour dye in bottom of container.

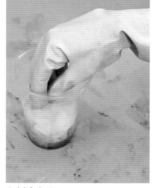

Add fabric.

Pour on second color of dye.

Scrunched fabric dyed with two colors

1B. Push the fabric into the container, pour in the first color, and move the fabric around to make sure the fabric is mostly colored. Pour the second color on top. At this point you can either leave the fabric alone or move it around a bit to get the colors to mix. Because the fabric is mostly covered with the first color, this approach will produce more blending of the second color. The more you move the fabric, the more the colors will blend.

Pour first color and move fabric around.

Add second color.

Scrunched fabric dyed with two colors

2. Let the fabric sit in the dye for 2 hours or more before washing (see Rinsing and Washing Dyed Fabric, page 13).

## MORE-THAN-TWO-COLOR DYEING

There is also more than one approach to dyeing more than two colors.

1A. Pour a little dye into the bottom of the container. Push part of the fabric into the container. Pour the second color of dye on top of the fabric. Use enough dye to saturate part of the fabric, but not so much that either color completely covers the fabric that is in the container. Push some more of the fabric into the container, and pour on a third color of dye. You can repeat this process for as much fabric as you have, adding as many colors as you like. At this point you can either leave the fabric alone or move it around a bit to get the colors to mix. With this approach, the colors will stay most distinct if you don't touch or move the fabric around. The more you move the fabric, the more the colors will blend.

Add first color.

Add second color.

Add third color.

Scrunched fabric dyed with several colors using container

1B. Pour dye directly on the fabric, and roll it around in your hands to make sure it is mostly colored. Pour the second color on top. Move the fabric around a bit to cover only portions of it. You can roll the fabric around in your hands again or just leave it as is. Continue this process with other colors. At this point you can either leave the fabric alone or move it around a bit more to get the colors to mix. With this approach, because the fabric is mostly covered with the first color, all the subsequent colors will blend with the first. The more you manipulate the fabric, the more all the colors will blend.

Add first color.

Add second color.

Add third color.

Scrunched fabric dyed with several colors using hands

2. Let the fabric sit in the dye for 2 hours or more before washing (see Rinsing and Washing Dyed Fabric, page 13).

## rolling

Rather than scrunching fabric into a container, you can roll it. The tighter the roll, the less dye will reach the inside of the roll. Folding or scrunching the folded fabric into a container can also introduce interesting patterns. You can start with white fabric or dye over a previously dyed piece of fabric.

1. Roll the fabric, and let it sit in the dye for several hours.

Roll fabric and place in dye.

2. Rinse the fabric well, and roll it up the other way, so that what was on the inside is now on the outside of the roll. Soak in a different color of dye for several hours.

Rinse and reroll fabric after it has been dyed once.

3. Let the fabric sit in the dye for 2 hours or more before washing (see Rinsing and Washing Dyed Fabric, page 13).

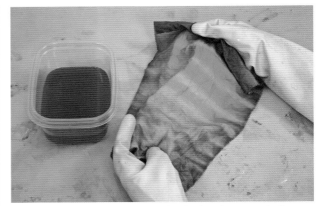
Rolled fabric after second color has been applied

## easy!

Some dyes that are made up of multiple colors will separate out, resulting in multiple colors on the fabric. The more the fabric is scrunched and the less it's moved around in the container, the more distinct the separation.

It's hard to predict which dye powders will do this. Black Cherry from Dharma Trading is one of my favorite separating colors.

Some dyes separate during dyeing process, producing several different colors on same fabric.

## Wet vs. Dry Fabric

You may be surprised to know that it can make a difference if the fabric is wet or dry when you dye it. Dry fabric actually results in smoother, softer patterns. The water in the wet fabric acts as a resist, resulting in sharper, more defined texture.

Same dye with different results, depending on whether dye process started with dry or wet fabric.

# Variations

**A. Scrunched fabrics (1 color)**

**B. Scrunched fabrics (2 colors)**

**C. Scrunched fabrics (3 colors)**

**D. Rolled fabrics**

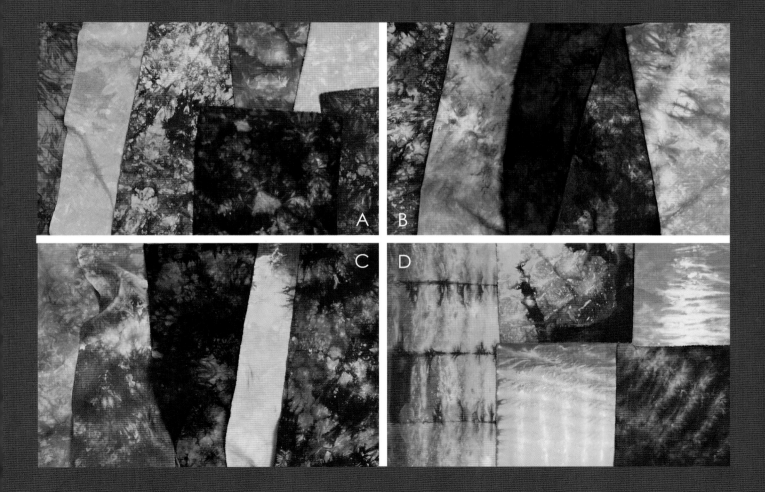

**MOSTLY SOLID:** *Sun and Stars*, 53″ × 60″, Lynn Koolish

**TEXTURED:** *Contraposed Curves*,
36″ × 36″, Lynn Koolish

**TEXTURED:** *Blue-Green Convergence*, 36″ × 36″,
Lynn Koolish (includes one commercially printed fabric,
using Ricky Tims's convergence technique)

mostly solid and textured dyeing gallery  **33**

**SOLID:** *Blue Blossoms on a Hot Day*, 18$\frac{1}{2}$″ × 21″, Becky Goldsmith, fabric dyed by Primrose Gradations

**MOSTLY SOLID AND TEXTURED:** *Leaves*, 23$\frac{1}{2}$″ × 26″, Lynn Koolish

**SOLID AND TEXTURED:** *Poppy Clock*, 14″ × 14″, Lynn Koolish. This clock is also shown in *Fast, Fun & Easy Creative Fabric Clocks* by Lynn Koolish, available from C&T Publishing.

**SOLID:** *Square in a Square Clock*, 18″ × 18″, Lynn Koolish. This clock is also shown in *Fast, Fun & Easy Creative Fabric Clocks* by Lynn Koolish, available from C&T Publishing.

# dyeing gradations

Whether you create a light-to-dark gradation within a single color or a gradation that goes from one color to another, hand-dyed gradations are versatile additions to your fabric stash.

# One-Color, Six-Step Gradation

## What You'll Need

- ☐ 6 quarter-yard pieces of fabric
- ☐ 6 containers (the larger the container, the more even the color will be)

  For mostly solid color, use 2-quart to 1-gallon containers; for more textured patterns, use pint to quart containers.

  For larger amounts of fabric, scale up the size of the container and the amount of dye accordingly.

### DYEING TIME

- ☐ 2 hours or longer

## How-Tos

### preparation

1. Use PFD fabric (see Cotton, page 6) or prewash your fabric to remove any finishing that may inhibit dyeing. Either plan to add soda ash to your dye mixture or use soda-soaked fabric (see Soda Ash, page 6). Start with wet or dry fabric.

2. Fill each container with warm water and 1 teaspoon of soda ash.

3. Stir to dissolve the soda ash.

4. Mix 1½ teaspoons of dye powder into 1 cup of warm water.

5. Add dye solution to each container as listed below, starting with the ½ teaspoon. The amounts listed are just starting points and can be adjusted as desired. Check your colors (see easy!, page 20). Mix up and add more dye to any of the containers to adjust the values before you add the fabric.

| CONTAINER | 1 | 2 | 3 | 4 | 5 | 6 |
|---|---|---|---|---|---|---|
| Color 1 | ½ tsp. | 1 tsp. | 1 Tbsp. | 2 Tbsp. | 4 Tbsp. | 8 Tbsp. |

Note: tsp. = teaspoon, Tbsp. = tablespoon, 16 tablespoons = 1 cup

### dyeing

1. Place a quarter-yard of fabric in each container. For solid colors, stir or agitate frequently, especially at the beginning of the dyeing time. For textured colors, don't disturb the fabrics after you've put them in the containers.

2. Let the fabric sit in the dye for 2 hours or more before washing (see Rinsing and Washing Dyed Fabric, page 13).

Place fabrics in containers.

One-color gradation

# Two-Color, Six-Step Gradation

## What You'll Need

- ☐ 6 quarter-yard pieces of fabric
- ☐ 6 containers (the larger the container, the more even the color will be)

    For mostly solid color, use 2-quart to 1-gallon containers; for more textured patterns, use pint to quart containers.

    For larger amounts of fabric, scale up the size of the container and the amount of dye accordingly.

# fun!

Selecting colors can be the most enjoyable part of the process (see Color, page 15). Analogous or other closely related colors will produce predictable and pleasing color gradations. Complementary and other contrasting colors will be more unpredictable but can be very interesting. Try some new color combinations and test them on paper (see easy!, page 20) before preparing the dye solutions.

## DYEING TIME

- ☐ 2 hours or longer

# How-Tos

## preparation

1. Fill each container with warm water and 1 teaspoon of soda ash.

2. Stir to dissolve the soda ash.

3. For each of the 2 colors, mix 1½ teaspoons of dye powder into 1 cup plus 1 tablespoon of warm water.

4. Add dye solution to each container as listed below. The amounts listed are just starting points and can be adjusted as desired. Check your colors (see easy!, page 20). Mix up and add more dye to any of the containers to adjust the values before you add the fabric.

| CONTAINER | 1 | 2 | 3 | 4 | 5 | 6 |
|---|---|---|---|---|---|---|
| Color 1 | 0 | 1 tsp. | 1 Tbsp. | 3 Tbsp. | 5 Tbsp. | 7 Tbsp. |
| Color 2 | 7 Tbsp. | 5 Tbsp. | 3 Tbsp. | 1 Tbsp. | 1 tsp. | 0 |
| Note: tsp. = teaspoon, Tbsp. = tablespoon, 16 tablespoons = 1 cup | | | | | | |

# easy!

## dyeing

**1.** Place the fabric in each container. For solid colors, stir or agitate frequently, especially at the beginning of the dyeing time. For textured colors, don't disturb the fabric after you've put it in the container.

Place fabric in containers.

**2.** Let the fabric sit in the dye for 2 hours or more before washing (see Rinsing and Washing Dyed Fabric, page 13).

# easy!

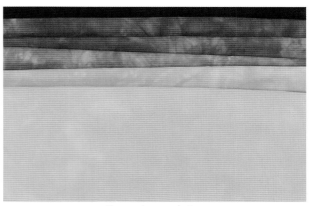

Two-color gradation

# Easy Three-Step Gradation

## What You'll Need

- ☐ 3 pieces of fabric

- ☐ 3 containers (the larger the container, the more even the color will be)

    For mostly solid color, use 1-gallon containers; for more textured patterns, use 1- to 2-cup containers.

For larger amounts of fabric, scale up the size of the container and the amount of dye accordingly.

**DYEING TIME**

- ☐ 2 hours or longer

| MOSTLY SOLID DYEING *AMOUNTS PER ¼ YARD OF FABRIC* | | | | |
|---|---|---|---|---|
| | DYE POWDER | SODA ASH* | SALT | CONTAINER |
| Light color | ¼–½ teaspoon | 1 teaspoon | 4 teaspoons | 1 gallon |
| Medium color | ½ teaspoon | 1 teaspoon | 4 teaspoons | 1 gallon |
| Dark color | 1 teaspoon | 1 teaspoon | 4 teaspoons | 1 gallon |
| TEXTURED DYEING *LOW-WATER IMMERSION, AMOUNTS PER ¼ YARD OF FABRIC* | | | | |
| | DYE POWDER | SODA ASH* | | CONTAINER |
| Light color | ⅛ teaspoon | 1 teaspoon | NA | 1–2 cups |
| Medium color | ¼ teaspoon | 1 teaspoon | NA | 1–2 cups |
| Dark color | ½ teaspoon | 1 teaspoon | NA | 1–2 cups |
| * Either plan to add soda ash to your dye mixture, or use soda-soaked fabric (see Soda Ash, page 6). | | | | |

# How-Tos

1. Mix the dyes as you would for a light, a medium, and a dark color as indicated on page 40.

2. Check your colors (see easy!, page 20). Mix up and add more dye to any of the containers to adjust the values before you add the fabric.

3. Place the fabric in each container.

4. Let the fabric sit in the dye for 2 hours or more before washing (see Rinsing and Washing Dyed Fabric, page 13).

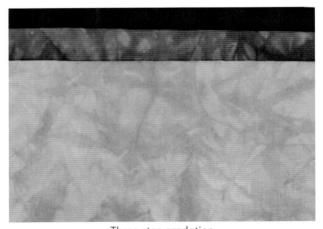

Three-step gradation

Place fabric in containers.

# Variations

**A. One-color, six-step gradations**

**B. Two-color, six-step gradations**

**C. One-color, three-step gradations**

# applying dye directly

Let out your inner artist. Applying dyes directly to fabric opens even more doors to unique fabric creations.

# What You'll Need

- ☐ PFD or prewashed fabric (see Cotton, page 6)
- ☐ Sodium alginate to thicken dyes (optional)
- ☐ Foam brushes
- ☐ Bristle brushes
- ☐ Squeeze bottles
- ☐ Spray bottles
- ☐ Plastic to cover fabric
- ☐ Optional: Large shallow plastic container (such as the trays designed to go under a washing machine or a refrigerator, or an under-the-bed storage box)

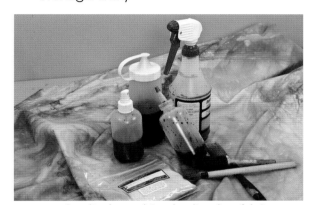

Supplies for applying dye directly to fabric

To determine the amount of dye and soda ash to use, you need to estimate how much fabric you will be covering with each color. For example, if you have 1 yard of fabric and are going to use four different colors, base your dye mixtures on ¼ yard of fabric. If you have 1 yard of fabric and are mostly using one color with a few accent colors, base your dye mixture on 1 yard of fabric for the main color and fractions of ¼ yard for the other colors. Adjust as needed.

## DYEING TIME

- ☐ Overnight

# How-Tos

In addition to dyeing fabric in containers, you can apply dye directly to fabric by painting, pouring, spraying, dribbling, squirting . . . you name it. The techniques in the next chapter (Dyeing Patterns) are also forms of direct application.

If you want your dyed designs to stay relatively distinct, start with dry fabric. If you want the designs to blend more, start with wet fabric.

| DIRECT APPLICATION *AMOUNTS PER 1 YARD OF FABRIC* | | | |
|---|---|---|---|
| | **DYE POWDER** | **SODA ASH\*** | **AMOUNT OF LIQUID\*\*** |
| Light color | ½ teaspoon | 1 tablespoon | 1–1½ cups |
| Medium color | 1 teaspoon | 1 tablespoon | 1–1½ cups |
| Dark color | 2 teaspoons | 1 tablespoon | 1–1½ cups |

| DIRECT APPLICATION *AMOUNTS PER ¼ YARD OF FABRIC* | | | |
|---|---|---|---|
| | **DYE POWDER** | **SODA ASH\*** | **AMOUNT OF LIQUID\*\*** |
| Light color | ¼ teaspoon | 1 teaspoon | ¼–½ cup |
| Medium color | ½ teaspoon | 1 teaspoon | ¼–½ cup |
| Dark color | 1 teaspoon | 1 teaspoon | ¼–½ cup |
| *\* Either plan to add soda ash to your dye mixture, or use soda-soaked fabric (see Soda Ash, page 6).* | | | |
| *\*\* If you plan to thicken the dye with sodium alginate, use water and prepared sodium alginate to get the desired thickness.* | | | |

# preparation

1. Use PFD fabric (see Cotton, page 6) or prewash your fabric to remove any finishing that may inhibit dyeing. Either plan to add soda ash to your dye mixture, or use soda-soaked fabric (see Soda Ash, page 6). This is a good time to use soda-soaked fabric so you can take your time applying the dyes. Start with wet or dry fabric.

2. Select a flat container based on the amount of fabric you have, or use a plastic-covered work surface.

3. Prepare the dye (see Direct Application chart, page 43, and Mixing Dye Solutions, page 11).

# pouring and blending

1. Arrange the fabric in the container or on a plastic-covered work surface.

2. Pour the dyes onto the fabric.

3. If you leave the poured dye alone, it will seep and blend some on its own. Or you can use your hands to blend the colors. The more you move the fabric around, the more the colors will blend.

Pour dye and leave it alone.

Dyes blended on their own

Pour dye and blend with hands.

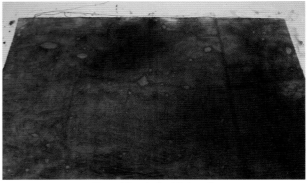

Dyes blended with hands

4. Cover the fabric with plastic, and let it sit overnight before washing (see Rinsing and Washing Dyed Fabric, page 13).

# easy!

You don't always have to start with white fabric. Add dimension by starting with previously dyed fabric.

## painting and squirting

1. Use sodium alginate (see Thickening Dyes, page 12) to thicken the dye. If you want the dye to spread, use just a little sodium alginate; if you want the dye to stay put, use more sodium alginate until the dye mixture is the consistency of honey.

2. Spread out the fabric in a shallow container or on a plastic-covered work surface.

3. Paint or squirt the thickened dyes onto the fabric.

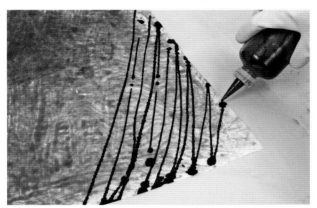

Squirt dye onto fabric with squeeze bottle.

Paint dye onto fabric.

4. Cover the fabric with plastic, and let it sit overnight before washing (see Rinsing and Washing Dyed Fabric, page 13).

## spraying

1. Pour the mixed dye into a spray bottle.

2. Spread out the fabric in a shallow container or on a plastic-covered work surface.

3. Spray the dye onto the fabric, blending the colors as desired.

Spray to blend colors . . .

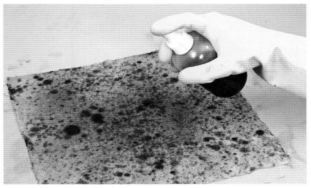

. . . or spray unevenly for more texture.

4. Cover the fabric with plastic, and let it sit overnight before washing (see Rinsing and Washing Dyed Fabric, page 13).

## easy!

When dyeing fabric with direct application, you'll probably be dyeing several pieces of fabric in one session. If they don't need to be in a container, simply stack them up with plastic in between each of the pieces of fabric.

# Variations

**A. Poured**    **B. Painted**

**C. Squirted**    **D. Sprayed**

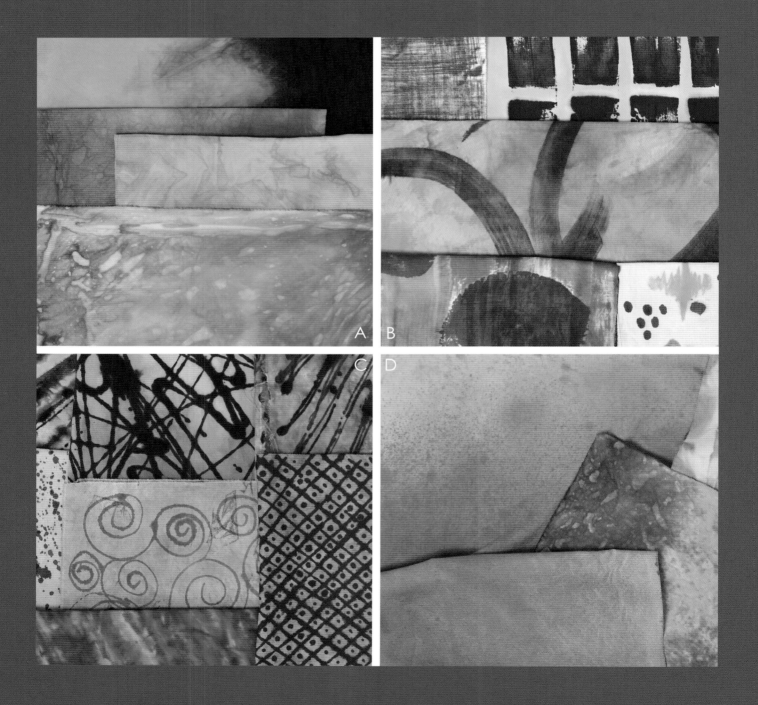

# dyeing
# patterns

There are many ways to pattern fabric with dyes. This chapter shows you just a few very easy techniques. Remember, you can apply dye to fabric any way you like. See what you can come up with.

# Shibori

There are many styles of Shibori, a Japanese dyeing technique. In general, fabric is folded, twisted, stitched, pleated, or otherwise manipulated so that patterns are created because dye can't reach some parts of the fabric. The patterns can be regular and symmetrical, or they can be totally random. You can be as deliberate or as random as you like. For the following style of Shibori, wrap fabric around a piece of large-diameter PVC pipe, and use rubber bands both to hold it to the pipe and to create patterns.

## What You'll Need

- ☐ PFD or prewashed fabric (see Cotton, page 6)
- ☐ PVC pipe
- ☐ Rubber bands
- ☐ Dye mixtures (see Mostly Solid Dyeing chart, page 22, if you will be immersing the fabric in a bucket, or Direct Application chart, page 43, if you will be applying the dye directly)

**DYEING TIME**

- ☐ 2 hours or longer

## How-Tos

### preparation

1. Use PFD fabric (see Cotton, page 6) or prewash your fabric to remove any finishing that may inhibit dyeing. Either plan to add soda ash to your dye mixture or use soda-soaked fabric (see Soda Ash, page 6). Start with wet or dry fabric.

2. Wrap the fabric around the pipe, and use rubber bands to secure it. Scrunch the fabric to one end of the pipe. Possible ways to wrap and secure the fabric include the following:

- ☐ Keep the fabric straight as you wrap it around the pipe.

- ☐ Place the fabric on a diagonal as you wrap it around the pipe.

- ☐ Pleat the fabric before you wrap it around the pipe.

- ☐ Twist the fabric as you wrap it around the pipe.

- ☐ Fold the fabric in patterns as you wrap it around the pipe.

Wrap and secure fabric.    Fabric ready for dye

### dyeing in a bucket

1. If you are using a single color, you can place the fabric-wrapped pipe in a bucket with dye.

2. Let the fabric sit in the dye for 2 hours or more before washing (see Rinsing and Washing Dyed Fabric, page 13).

### applying dye directly to fabric

1. If you want to use multiple colors at one time, paint or squirt dye onto the wrapped fabric. Thickened dye (see Thickening Dyes, page 12) will stay where you put it; thin dye will run and blend more.

Paint thickened dye onto fabric.

2. Cover the fabric with plastic, and let it sit overnight before washing (see Rinsing and Washing Dyed Fabric, page 13).

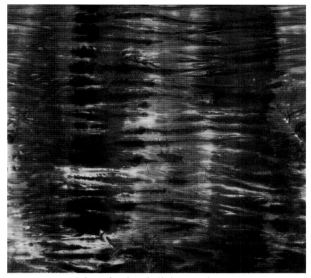

Fabric dyed with Shibori technique

# Folding

Folding fabric and dipping it in dye creates interesting repeat patterns.

## What You'll Need

☐ PFD or prewashed fabric (see Cotton, page 6)

☐ Dye mixtures (see Textured Dyeing, Low-Water Immersion chart, page 26).

### DYEING TIME

☐ 2 hours or longer

## How-Tos

### preparation

1. Think about the types of patterns you want—lines that go at right angles, diagonal lines, lines that are parallel, lines that intersect.

2. Fold the fabric. For diagonal lines, make sure the fabric has at least one fold on the diagonal.

3. If needed, use a rubber band to keep the fabric from unfolding.

### dyeing

1. Dip the folded fabric into the dye. If you want thin lines, use just a bit of dye in the bottom of a container. If you want thicker lines, use more dye. The longer the fabric sits in the dye, the more it will wick up into the fabric.

2. Try dipping one edge into one color of dye and other edges into other colors.

Dyeing folded fabric

3. Let the fabric sit in the dye for 2 hours or more before washing (see Rinsing and Washing Dyed Fabric, page 13).

# fun!

To get a preview of how your fabric will dye, fold the fabric, and press or finger-press the folds. Unfold the fabric, and look at the pressed lines. These will be the main lines of your dyed fabric.

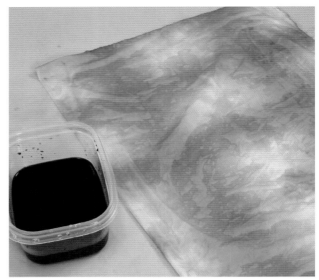
Fabric unfolded

## Monoprinting

Monoprinting is another easy way to get unique patterns on fabric. By applying thickened dyes (see Thickening Dyes, page 12) to a smooth surface instead of the fabric, you can create one-of-a-kind designs and patterns.

## What You'll Need

- ☐ PFD or prewashed fabric (see Cotton, page 6)

- ☐ 18″ × 18″ square (or larger) of vinyl, such as Quilter's Vinyl (see Resources, page 62), a smooth counter, or a piece of Plexiglas

- ☐ Assorted scrapers, notched spreaders, and other marking utensils

- ☐ Brayer (optional)

- ☐ Dye mixtures (see Direct Application chart, page 43)—I recommend using soda-soaked fabric so you have more time to experiment.

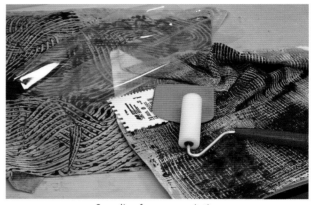
Supplies for monoprinting

### DYEING TIME

- ☐ Overnight

## How-Tos

### preparation

1. Mix dyes, and thicken with sodium alginate (see Thickening Dyes, page 12).

2. For larger pieces of fabric, apply dyes to an old work counter or plastic-covered table. For smaller pieces of fabric, apply dyes to a square of vinyl or Plexiglas.

# dyeing

1. Create your design. Either place fabric on the dye, or if you are using vinyl, flip the vinyl over onto the fabric. You can try any of the following:

☐ Use your hands to "finger-paint."

☐ Use a paintbrush, squeeze bottle, or spray bottle.

☐ Apply dye; then use a notched spreader to create series of parallel lines.

☐ Apply the dye to the vinyl, and then fold in half, pressing the 2 sides together. When you unfold the vinyl, you'll have interesting textures.

☐ Any combination of the above or anything else you can think of.

Create design on vinyl.

2. Use a brayer or your hands, and rub the fabric or vinyl to make sure the dye is transferred to the fabric.

Lift fabric to check transfer of thickened dye.

3. Cover the fabric with plastic, and let it sit overnight before washing (see Rinsing and Washing Dyed Fabric, page 13).

NOTE: When you are using vinyl, the type of vinyl and how much it has been used will affect how the dye will sit on the surface. Newer vinyl often resists the dye, so dyes will bead up, and you will get different textures than you will with vinyl that has been used for a while.

Used vinyl (left) and new vinyl (right)

# fast!

A fast way to get great patterns on fabric is to use a rag roller. These rollers are used for faux painting, and many hardware stores carry them. Use thickened dyes (see Thickening Dyes, page 12) for the best patterns.

Rag roller and dyed fabric

# Variations

**A. Shibori**

**B. Folded**

**C. Monoprinted**

**D. Rolled with rag roller**

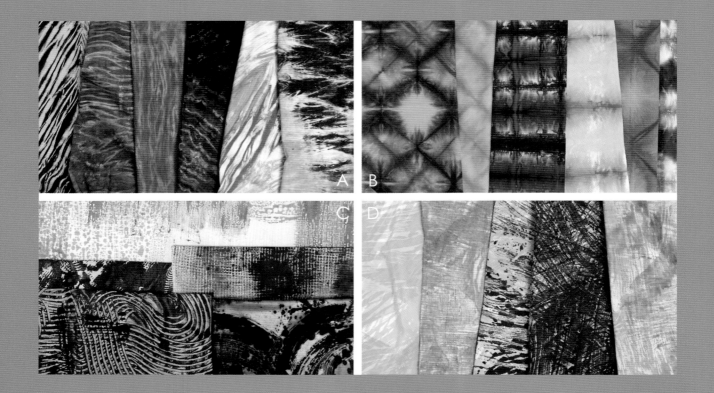

# dyeing silk and wool

Think of the possibilities: softer-than-soft silk quilts, floaty silk scarves, socks knit with hand-dyed wool, and scarves made from luscious silk ribbon.

# What You'll Need

- ☐ PFD or prewashed silk (see Fabrics, page 6) or wool
- ☐ Distilled white vinegar
- ☐ Pyrex or other microwave-safe container
- ☐ Microwave oven

## DYEING TIME

- ☐ 6 to 30 minutes (depending on the wattage of your microwave oven)

**NOTE:** After you have used a microwave for dyeing, you should never use it for food. Inexpensive microwaves are readily available, so take this opportunity to get a new microwave for the kitchen, and use your old one for dyeing.

| STEAMING IN THE MICROWAVE *AMOUNTS PER 1 YARD OF FABRIC OR 1 SKEIN OF YARN* | | |
|---|---|---|
| | **DYE POWDER** | **WATER** |
| Light color | ½ teaspoon | 1–2 cups* |
| Medium color | 1 teaspoon | 1–2 cups* |
| Dark color | 2 teaspoons | 1–2 cups* |
| STEAMING IN THE MICROWAVE *AMOUNTS PER ¼ YARD OF FABRIC* | | |
| | **DYE POWDER** | **WATER** |
| Light color | ⅛ teaspoon | ¼–½ cup* |
| Medium color | ¼ teaspoon | ¼–½ cup* |
| Dark color | ½ teaspoon | ¼–½ cup* |
| *\* If you are using multiple colors, use less water for each color.* | | |

# How-Tos

**NOTE:** Silk can be dyed in two ways: It can be dyed just like cotton fabric, using soda ash to fix the dye, or it can be dyed in a microwave oven, using steam and vinegar to set the dye. For textured results, you can use either process. This chapter will focus on a quick steam-setting microwave method that works best for textured results. To achieve solid or mostly solid colors use the Mostly Solid Dyeing method, pages 21–23.

## preparation

1. Use PFD silk (see Fabrics, page 6) or prewash your fabric (or ribbon, scarves, or other textiles) to remove any finishing that may inhibit dyeing. For wool yarn, make sure it is free of substances, such as lanolin, that will inhibit the dye process.

# easy!

For yarn, tie skeins in at least six places.

**2.** Soak the silk or wool in a mixture of ⅔ vinegar and ⅓ water. The vinegar-and-water mixture is reusable, so save it in a clearly marked container.

# fast!

**3.** Prepare the dye (see Steaming in the Microwave chart, page 54, and Mixing Dye Solutions, page 11). Remember, don't add any soda ash.

## dyeing

**1.** Pour the dye over the wet silk or wool. As with other dyeing techniques, if you are using multiple colors, the more you manipulate the fibers, the more the dyes will blend.

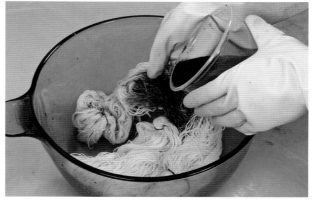

Pour dye over fabric or yarn.

Yarn after all colors are added

Dyed yarn

2. Make sure there is enough liquid in the container so that steam will be produced throughout the entire steaming time. If you aren't sure, you can place a small glass jar of water in the container to generate more steam.

3. The amount of time needed to steam will depend on the wattage of your microwave oven. In general, more time is better than less time, but keep an eye on your project—if there isn't enough liquid, the fabric will scorch or burn.

4. To get a more even distribution of color when dyeing larger amounts of fabric or yarn, stop the microwave halfway through the allotted time, and *very carefully* move the fabric or yarn around in the container so that the part that was at the top is now on the bottom.

GUIDELINES FOR STEAMING (adjust as needed for your microwave and for larger amounts of fabric or yarn):

☐ Small scarf or ¼ yard of fabric: 10 minutes on high

☐ ½ yard of fabric: 20 minutes on high

☐ Skein of yarn or yard of fabric: 30 minutes on high

5. When the time is up, let the fabric or yarn sit and cool for 15 minutes or longer.

# easy!

You can dye wool either before or after it has been knit or crocheted.

# rinsing and washing

1. Rinse the silk or wool in cold water first. Then start washing the fabric or yarn with warm water and Synthrapol or detergent.

2. Continue washing until no more color comes out in the water. A good approach is to leave the fabric or yarn soaking in water and Synthrapol or detergent for 15 minutes, and come back later to rinse. Do this as many times as needed.

3. If it feels like you can't get all the excess dye out, you've either used too much dye or haven't steamed enough. You can resoak the fabric or yarn in the water and vinegar mixture, and steam it again to see if that helps, or you can continue to soak and wash until the wash water runs clear.

> **NOTE:** If you are working with wool, wash gently and don't use hot water, or you may end up with felt.

# drying

☐ For silk or wool fabric, wrap the fabric in a towel to blot excess water, then hang it to dry. Drying in a dryer can be too abrasive and leave marks on the fabric. The fabric may feel a little stiff when dry—this is helpful when dyeing silk for piecing. If you want your silk to be very soft and silky, add a little bit of fabric softener to the final rinse.

☐ For a yarn or knit or crocheted item, wrap the item in a towel to blot excess water, then place it on a towel to dry.

# easy!

Plan to do laundry after you dye—placing the yarn on top of a hot dryer will speed up the drying process.

# Variations

A. Dyed silks, textured (one color)　　B. Dyed silks, multicolored

C. Socks knit with hand-dyed wool　　D. Dyed wool yarn and socks
　　　　　　　　　　　　　　　　　　　(knit by Becky Goldsmith)

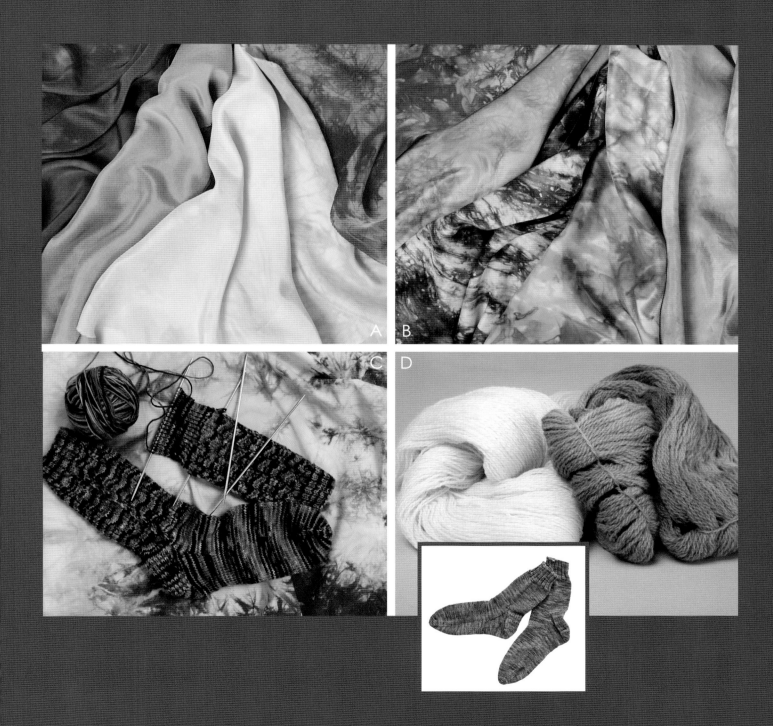

A

B

C

D

**PATTERNS:** *Heart Beet,* 48˝ × 54˝, Lynn Koolish, quilted by Laura Lee Fritz (includes some commercially printed fabric)

**SHIBORI, SOLID, AND TEXTURED:** *Birds of Paradise,* 33$\frac{1}{2}$″ × 53″, Lynn Koolish (includes hand-dyed and commercially printed fabric)

**MIXED TECHNIQUES IN SILK:** *Going with the Flow,* 36″ × 44″, Lynn Koolish

**THREE-STEP GRADATION:** *Twilight,* 34$\frac{1}{4}$″ × 34$\frac{1}{4}$″, Helen Frost. This quilt is also shown in the book *Radiant Sunshine & Shadow* by Helen Frost and Catherine Skow from C&T Publishing.

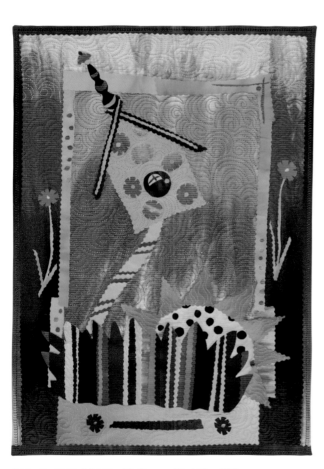

**BLEND AND SOLID:** *Birdhouse #8,* 14″ × 22″, Laura Wasilowski, fabric dyed by Laura Wasilowski/ArtFabrik

**MICROWAVE SILK:** *Silk Pinwheels,* 40″ × 48″, designed by Lynn Koolish, made by Diana Malone, quilted by Ramona Sorenson for Corn Wagon Quilt Company

Once you have the supplies to dye, why stop at fabric? Spice up your wardrobe and make it uniquely yours, or just update it with new colors. Liven up your dining room table with linens for every occasion. And don't forget silk scarves—my favorite accessory. They are quick and easy gifts that everyone loves.

### SCARVES

Premade scarves, hemmed and ready to dye, are easy to find (see Resources, page 62) and quick to dye (see Dyeing Silk and Wool, page 53). Scarves can also be knit from dyed silk ribbon.

### SHIRTS (COTTON)

What an easy way to liven up your wardrobe! And they make great gifts. Dye for texture (see Textured Dyeing, page 25), or apply the dyes directly for blends (see Applying Dye Directly, page 42).

### T-SHIRTS AND SOCKS

Perk up an old faded tee or buy new white ones and dye them to match your favorite pants, shorts, or skirts. Dye them using any technique. Socks can also be dyed using any technique.

# resources

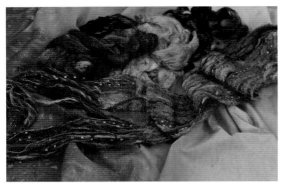

**SILK ROVING FOR FIBER PROJECTS**

Silk roving (see Resources) adds a soft, luxurious touch to fiber projects. Dye silk roving in the microwave (see Dyeing Silk and Wool, page 53).

**SILK RIBBON, RICKRACK, AND TWILL TAPE**

Perfect for knitting (see knit silk ribbon scarf, page 61) and for embellishing clothing, quilts, scrapbooks, and altered art. Paint on color (see Painting and Squirting, page 45) or dip in a container (see Dyeing in Buckets, page 23).

**LINENS**

Do you have an old cedar chest full of mismatched and spotted linens? They dye beautifully, and you can pick colors for any occasion. Use any technique.

## DYES, AUXILIARIES, FABRIC

### Creative Impressions

Silk ribbon, 100% cotton rickrack, and twill tape
www.creativeimpressions.com
719-596-4860
Order by phone or online.

### Dharma Trading

Dyes, auxiliaries, PFD fabric, premade clothing to dye, silk ribbon, silk roving, and much more
www.dharmatrading.com
800-542-5227
Order by phone, online, or at the Dharma Trading store in San Rafael, CA.

### Duncan Enterprises

Tulip and Rainbow Rock dyes
www.duncancrafts.com
Available at craft chain stores and Wal-Mart.

### Jacquard Products

Dyes and auxiliaries
www.jacquardproducts.com
800-442-0455
Check the website for retailers.

### Kaufman Fabrics

PFD cotton and cotton/silk blends
www.robertkaufman.com
800-877-2066
Check the website for retailers.

### Pro Chemical & Dye

Dyes, auxiliaries, PFD fabric, and workshops
www.prochemical.com
800-228-9393
Order by phone or online.

### RJR Fabrics

PFD cotton and silk
www.rjrfabrics.com
800-422-5426
Check the website for retailers.

### Silk Connection

PFD cotton and silk fabric, scarves, and ties
www.silkconnection.com
800-442-0455
Order by phone or online.

## BOOKS ON DYEING

*Color by Accident* and *Color by Design* by Ann Johnston (www.annjohnston.net), published by Ann Johnston

*Complex Cloth* by Jane Dunnewold (www.artclothstudios.com), published by Martingale

**For a list of other fine books from C&T Publishing, ask for a free catalog:**

C&T Publishing, Inc.

P.O. Box 1456
Lafayette, CA 94549
800-284-1114
ctinfo@ctpub.com
www.ctpub.com

**For quilting supplies:**

Cotton Patch

1025 Brown Avenue
Lafayette, CA 94549
800-835-4418 or
925-283-7883
CottonPa@aol.com
www.quiltusa.com

# about the author

Sewing has been a constant in Lynn's life ever since her mother taught her to sew when she was old enough to sit at a sewing machine. Lynn has worked in a number of careers but was thrilled to finally settle down with quilting in the 1990s.

Lynn works in a variety of styles and loves experimenting with new ideas, materials, and techniques. She works full time editing quilting books and teaches a variety of surface design and quilting classes. Her quilts have appeared in books, magazines, and local and national quilt shows. Visit Lynn's website at www.lynnkoolish.com.

**Lynn Koolish**

**ALSO BY LYNN KOOLISH:**

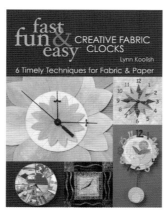
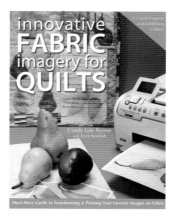

# Great Titles from C&T PUBLISHING

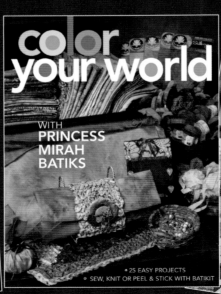